Angels & Addicts

Living the Life you were meant to Live

Angels & Addicts

Published by aah-ha! Books, Inc.
http://www.starwater.com

aah-ha! Books are published by aah-ha! Books, Inc.
Its trademark, consisting of the words aah-ha! Books and logo,
are registered in U.S. Patent and Trademark Office
Library of Congress Catalog Card # 98-86370

ISBN 1-889853-51-8

PRINTED IN THE UNITED STATES OF AMERICA

6 8 9 7 5

Dedicated to the
Angel and the addict within each of us.

Introduction

In 1984 I experienced what I know now to be a spiritual rebirth. And what precipitated this rebirth was the death of my son Gregory who died at three and a half months old of SIDS (Sudden Infant Death Syndrome.)

With his death, the "me" I knew, died. I did not die physically but what did die was all that I had ever believed in, all that I thought I was.

A big part of me died with him in the ambulance on that cold, December day. I was empty. Suddenly nothing made sense.

Then an Angel came to help me walk the path back to the living. She guided me. She spoke to me, until I could hear again, until I could heal. It was then that I began to rebuild my life and set off on my journey.

Ten years later, she suggested I go back to school. At the time I was looking for meaning and trying to live my purpose. But when the spiritual voice that I trusted told me to study and become an addictions counselor, I fought it.

This was the last job I had ever envisioned myself having. I reminded myself that this was God's will, not mine. So I moaned, but I went.

The addictions course I chose was based on a Twelve Step Program.

I was taught that this twelve step program would be used as a way to recover from the "disease" of Alcoholism and Addiction.

As the training continued, I began to understand why I had been guided in this direction.

Bill Wilson, founder of AA and the twelve steps had also had a spiritual awakening. Because of my own experience, it became obvious to me that the twelve steps were divinely inspired.

God's will, not Bill's. Bill Wilson had been given a map to Spiritual growth and rebirth.

Later, when I became a counselor I learned more about each step and I began to watch the "process of recovery" unfold in my clients.

In the middle of running a group one day something amazing occurred to me. I realized that after my son died I had gone through each and every one of these steps. They were the "process" that the Angel Janith took me through to guide me back to the land of the living.

I had been part of this program but not as a recovering Alcoholic or Addict. I had gone through them as a mother in grief.

With this recognition "Recovery" took on a whole new meaning for me. Recovery now meant "to recover the soul and the life you were born to live."

Angels and Addicts is the coming together of that recognition.

The twelve steps are not only for Alcoholics, Addicts or mothers in grief. They are for all of us.

These twelve steps are the map by which the Angels can guide us. They can lead us to our final destination: the purpose we were born to live.

Each step can take us through our own spiritual awakening, to meet the Angel who can help bring us back to life.

It is a clear and easy way to walk a path of change and spirituality. And it is with a sincere and open heart that I offer them to you.

In order to use this book with the steps and meditations most effectively, I would like to offer some suggestions.

If you plan to work alone: Each of these steps can be focused on for short or long periods of time. I've found it works best if I focus on "Step One" as the theme of the day for a given period of time:

one day, one week, one month. You will find your own rhythm. The longer you dedicate to each step, the more understanding you will receive from it.

The "Angel" meditations can be read into a tape recorder in your own voice or you can work with a friend. You can also take turns reading it to each other. Please take your time and read them slowly. Only use the corresponding Angel meditation for whatever step you're on. Stay with that step and that meditation for as long as you decide, until you are ready to move on.

For Counselors or anyone working in a group situation, I've found these steps and meditations are even more effective. The meditations can be read by the facilitator during the beginning of the session. Your group can focus on the "step for the week" then when you gather again, the group can discuss the difficulties or benefits and effects it has had on their lives.

All of the meditations are available on tape from aah-ha! books if you find that you need them.

Good Luck on your Journey !!!

Teri

The Twelve Steps

1- We admitted we were powerless over alcohol— that our lives had become unmanageable.

2 - Came to believe that a Power greater than ourselves could restore us to sanity.

3 - Made a decision to turn our will and our lives over to the care of God, as we understood him.

4 - Made a searching and fearless moral inventory of ourselves.

5 - Admitted to God, ourselves, and to another human being the exact nature of our wrongs.

6 - Were entirely ready to have God remove all these defects of character.

7 - Humbly asked God to remove our shortcomings.

8 - Made a list of all persons we had harmed, and became willing to make amends to them all.

9 - Made direct amends to such people wherever possible, except when to do so would injure them or others.

10 - Continued to take personal inventory and when we were wrong promptly admitted it.

11 - Sought through prayer and meditation to improve our conscious contact with God, as we understood Him, praying only for knowledge of His will for us and the power to carry that out.

12 - Having had a spiritual awakening as a result of these steps, we tried to carry this message to alcoholics, and to practice these principles in all our affairs.

With two easy modifications, the twelve steps apply to all of us. Watch! Change the word alcohol in the first step to "our old self." Next change the word Alcoholics to "others" in the last step. And like magic these steps become our road map to the Divine.

Angels

Angels of Death
The Angel of Vision
The Angel of Recognition
The Angel of Connection

Angels of Discovery
The Angel of Truth
The Angel of Forgiveness
The Angel of Process

Angels of Birth
The Angel of Justice
The Angel of Peace
The Angel of Dignity

Angels of Healing
The Angel of Compassion
The Angel of Communication
The Angel of Purpose

An Angel is given
for each step that you take
Walking back to the living
restoring your faith

An Angel is watching
each step that you take
to reclaim the purpose
you were born to create

An Angel protects
with each step that you take
erases old patterns
and past mistakes

An Angel rejoices
in each step that you take
Another soul has been
saved before it's too late . . .

Table of Contents

Angel of Vision

The Angel of Vision is here to see
who you were really meant to be.
In all the confusion, with all the pain
this Angel is here to try to explain.

Step One

> **We admitted that we were powerless over our old self, that our lives had become unmanageable.**

It is so easy in today's world to become numb, to follow routine in all our actions, choices and relationships. We no longer feel fully alive. We rush to finish all that we must, forgetting to see, touch, taste, smell and feel the moments. We live this way, whether we want to or not.

We forget that we have choice. That we don't have to feel stressed, that we can take the long way home.

This first step helps to make us aware that we are powerless over our old destructive patterns, our old wounds, or unhappy childhoods. We seem unaware that we can let them go.

Step One simply states our lives have become unmanageable. This means our life is not what we want it to be and we are powerless to change it unless we begin to see how stuck we are in our old patterns and ideas.

Step one is an ending - but it is also a beginning.

Notes

Meditation
Meeting the Angel of Vision

Get comfortable and close your eyes. See your-self in a safe place, this could be the beach, a special room or the mountains. Take a few deep breaths knowing you are breathing out all of your stress.

You are only in this moment - in your safe place-letting everything else go.

Now see yourself sitting peacefully in your room or landscape. From down the path comes a being of light and as she comes closer, she gets clearer. You feel safe.

Soon you can see this beautiful Angel of light and she is holding what looks like a crystal ball in her hands. It seems to be floating between her hands as a bubble would. You feel a strange sense of calm as she stands before you.

You can feel how compassionate and caring this Angel is. She begins to show you the crystal ball, the crystal seems to be showing you scenes from your life. Watch now as this Angel shares her vision of your past.

With each scene a new color surrounds the crystal ball. These visions are of all the old behaviors and ways that no longer serve you.

The parts of you that need to be "let go" so you can become more.

The Angel now is holding her hands over the crystal and you know it is done. You have seen the need to let go of all that isn't working for you in your life and you are grateful. When you open your eyes you feel peaceful and alive.

Angel of Recognition

The Angel of Recognition only asks us to say
there may be a God who could change our old ways.
In admitting there may be a higher place
we leave room for the new to fill this space.

Step Two

> **We came to believe that a Power greater than ourselves could restore us to sanity.**

Think about it. We run around between work, family, chores, shopping, more work, and then we drop into bed, too late and exhausted. We don't even have time to dream! We sleep a quick sleep before the alarm rings again, too soon. If this is not insanity, what is?

The beginning of understanding step two is to slow down and recognize that there is a greater power than ourselves. An expanded reality exists and a bigger plan is unfolding as we are running through our lives.

It reminds us that this Power could restore us to sanity if we slow down long enough to recognize the existence of a Grand Plan and a Master Planner.

Somehow, just recognizing this makes us more sane. It puts our lives in perspective, helps us to regain some balance and maybe even have a conversation with our loved ones or play with our kids.

When a Higher Power exists we can take time to live and dream.

Notes

Meditation
Meeting the Angel of Recognition

Close your eyes and take a deep breath. With each breath you feel more relaxed. You are getting ready to go on a journey. You feel a light presence, first subtle then stronger, more loving and warm. Continue breathing peacefully, fully.

See yourself walking on a dirt path through a beautiful rose garden. The sun is shining, the sky is blue, only a few fluffy white clouds dot the sky. You notice all the different colors of the roses. Up ahead you see a bench to sit on and you go to it, sit and relax.

As you sit, you again feel this presence of light near you - warm and loving. You look around and you see the rose garden, the sun, the clouds. Small animals come to greet you - a rabbit, a fox and some squirrels. You look into their eyes. God is there and you feel the presence again.

Now you decide to walk down the path toward where you began. Birds fly overhead and a butterfly lands on your shoulder. You feel part of a world created out of love. It is good. All is right. *(pause for a few minutes)*

You are back where you began and when ready you open your eyes - *knowing.*

Angel of Connection

*The Angel of Connection only asks you to feel
the presence of light so loving, so real.
To make this connection each and every day
she asks that you get down on your knees and pray.*

Step Three

> **We made a decision to turn our will and our lives over to the care of God as we understand him.**

Step three is the most complex but simple step there is. Turning our will over to God "as we understand him" calls us to pray for our purpose in this life.

We don't have to know our God completely. We can begin by being confused and unsure about God and the place God holds in our lives. As long as we begin, the journey will continue.

We don't need to know where the path will lead, we must only be willing to walk it.

Making a decision to turn our will over means only that we made the decision - no more, no less. One step at a time is how this journey is taken. Give yourself time and space to begin to know your God.

The serenity prayer is a wonderful way to begin. Saying this prayer reminds us to make the *decision* to turn our will over on a moment to moment basis, each and every day.

Serenity Prayer

God, grant me the serenity to accept the things I cannot change. The courage to change the things I can and the wisdom to know the difference.

. . . .

Acceptance, Courage, Wisdom.
Nothing wrong with that!

Meditation
Meeting the Angel of Connection

Close your eyes and breathe in through your nose and out through your mouth. With each breath you feel more at peace knowing that you are blowing out all stress and anxiety. Breathing in peace and light.

This moment is for you and no one else. Continue to breathe normally as you see yourself in front of a silver staircase that winds up toward the clouds. As you look up you cannot see where the staircase ends. You begin walking up.

With each step you take you feel more protected, more loved, more at peace. As you reach the top few steps you notice a brilliant light coming from behind the clouds. You feel great joy as you reach the top step.

There before you stands the most beautiful majestic Angel you have ever seen. She welcomes you. She seems happy to see that you've made it this far.

She gives you a gift to bring back with you on your journey. Look at this gift. Notice what it is. You thank her for your present, and begin to go back down the stairs knowing that at anytime you can climb the silver staircase again and meet the Angel of connection.

When you feel ready open your eyes.

Angel of Truth

The Angel of Truth will show you the way
to open your heart to a magical day.
This Angel is true, she understands you
Give her a chance and try a new dance.

Step Four

> **Made a searching and fearless inventory
> of ourselves.**

The Angel of truth talks of a new dance. The dance she is speaking of is learning to see ourselves in an honest way: the good, the bad and the ugly, all without judgement and without punishing ourselves.

This step is a tricky one because we want to honestly look at ourselves but not for the purpose of judging ourselves, rather to see what we can use as tools to work with and which tools we've used that no longer serve us.

The only way for us to become who we want to be is to know who we are now. Then we can make a choice as to which aspects we find valuable and which we do not.

In the spiritual world, anger is not good or bad. Happiness is not good or bad. It just "is." Learning from and going though our emotions is what will help us change and grow.

Notes

Meditation
Meeting the Angel of Truth

This meeting would best take place in a quiet room, where you are not going to be interrupted for some time.

When you find a comfortable place, close your eyes, relax and take some deep breaths. Finding your center, that place of peace within you, continue to take slow deep breaths.

When you are relaxed, see yourself inside an empty room. The walls are white, no color or windows or doors in this room.

Sit in the middle of this empty room and notice how you are feeling.

The Angel of Truth now enters your empty white room and begins to point at the walls. Your emotions are the paint and objects that will fill this room, they will add color - not good or bad color, just color.

As the Angel points to the walls, you notice they become a light green. Next a chair appears and then a couch, a coffee table and a rug, notice what colors they are.

This is your "living" room and all that you are. All that you have ever been become objects in this room. Take a moment and watch what your room fills up with. Notice how you feel.

Look at the shapes, styles, colors and positions of the objects.

The Angel stands with you, supporting you as your living room reveals itself. Notice how you are feeling at this time. Look around at all you are and all you have created.

You may like some of the objects that fill your room and other objects you may not. It's O.k.

Feel at peace as you look around - just noticing and when you are ready you may open your eyes knowing that at anytime you can return to renovate your room of "living."

(hint) If you feel stuck on your journey - go to your room and rearrange some of the furniture or have a yard sale, then watch what happens!

Angel of Forgiveness

*The Angel of forgiveness leads you back to yourself
she hands you a mirror down from the shelf
she blows off the dust and wipes it clean
so you can see what it really does mean.*

Step Five

> *Admitted to God, ourselves and to another human being the exact nature of our wrongs.*

This is an important step - it can teach us a lot. People see events in different ways. Sometimes we feel we have done something wrong or hurt someone when others do not see it that way. We then have an opportunity to see the situation from another point of view.

When we admit to ourselves and to God the wrongs we feel we have done, when we face ourselves, we disempower the "demons" within. The secret is out. We are not perfect, and we allow ourselves our human mistakes, and own our human nature.

We then experience God, ourselves and others in a new way. Then others are free to love us with all our imperfections.

It is with that acknowledgement that we step into the world where everyone has past wrongs and is imperfect. It is only then that we can become part of the human race. Now we are connected and included in our world.

Once we can accept who we are, we feel less of a struggle internally and become more peaceful.

Notes

Meditation
Meeting the Angel of Forgiveness

Get ready to feel better than you have in a long time. Come and meet the Angel of forgiveness.

Close your eyes and get comfortable. As you breathe begin to see a blue light above your head and allow it to gently move down through your head and shoulders.

You're feeling warm and peaceful as this healing light moves down through your chest. Blue peaceful light moves down now through your abdomen and legs, relaxing, healing.

Blue light down now through your ankles and feet.

You are now surrounded by this blue, safe, healing light.

See yourself in a meadow. It is a beautiful day, the sun is shining. There is a warm breeze blowing.

The Angel of forgiveness is walking toward you and you are filled with love.

The Angel stands in front of you and she hands

you a mirror. She explains, "This is the mirror of *self reflection,*" and asks that you hold it up to see your face. Look into this mirror.

What do you see? What are you feeling?

The Angel now reaches out her hand and puts it gently on your shoulder. You feel an over-whelming gratitude for her presence. She smiles and takes the mirror, letting you know you have done well. It is enough for today.

When you are ready you can open your eyes.

Angel of Process

The Angel of Process takes one step at a time
having patience, while you tow the line.
The Angel of Process is a sister to pain
she knows the circle must begin again.

Step Six

> **We're entirely ready to have God
> remove all these defects of character.**

Being ready doesn't mean this happens all at once. It only means that we are *willing* to let go of these defects. Once our hand is open, God can take them from us. God will not wrestle with a closed fist.

Who we are is a choice.

When this occurs we have agreed to empty out old useless emotions that no longer serve who we are today and who we are trying to become.

When a glass is full we cannot add anything until it is emptied out. Then and only then can we fill our glass with what we wish; not what was put there by others during our growing up.

We can give all old wounds and resentments to God just by one intention to give them away.

You may want to write a list of what you consider your "defects" and then, in a ceremony, light a candle and say a prayer that you will be released from these old wounds that created defenses that you no longer need.

Notes

Meditation
Meeting the Angel of Process

Find a place to lie down. As you close your eyes, breathe deeply, peacefully. This moment in time is yours to be relaxed and free from all worry. Clear your mind and if a thought comes, don't fight it, just watch it pass by.

See a green light above your head that flows easily down, healing, a green light moves down through your head and shoulders. It is as if you are an open vessel and the green light flows down through your neck and chest as a river would, peacefully flowing down now through your stomach and abdomen pushing away any stress or tension that you are holding in your body. This green healing light flows down now through your pelvic area, legs, ankles and feet. You are surrounded with the divine green light of healing.

You now see a ship and you climb in. Notice what your ship is made of. You are floating down the *River of Process*. As you float, the water is calm, the landscape around you is somewhat rocky. The sun is shining - you feel the warmth on your face. As you look to the sky you see an eagle flying overhead. The Angel of Process is sitting on a rock up ahead and she gets into your ship and sits in the back as you continue to navigate your way down the River of Process.

Looking at the shore, you see past events in your life. People you have met, experiences that have made you who you are today. The Angel is with you and you are safe.

Take a moment to notice which people and events are important as you watch them play out a scene on the shore.

You continue floating slowly by each scene, noticing how your defects developed and why you needed them to survive.

The ship has returned now to the shore where you began. You step out onto land and thank the Angel for riding with you, knowing that at any time you can return to this ship and the river of process to continue your journey. You have done well.

When you're ready you can come back into this room and open your eyes. You may want to write down what you experienced.

Angel of Justice

The Angel of Justice reveals the Plan
As she swirls and twirls throughout the new land.
Showing each soul In Technicolor Dreams
How life flows from Divine Streams.

Step Seven

> ***Humbly asked God to remove
> our shortcomings.***

Now we know some of our shortcomings. We pray to God to take them from us. In doing this, we are asking God to give us the strength to move past our fears and become a more responsible, conscious person in the world.

Once our shortcomings are removed, we are able to do more, see more and become more.

Shortcomings within us are the aspects that hold us back from living our life's purpose. Leaving these old patterns of behavior behind, gives us the power to move in new directions in our life.

"We ask humbly" because we know that "grace" is the only thing that can help us to reunite with the *child of potential* - the child who was born without these shortcomings, before the world helped us to create them. And we understand that we created them out of a need for protection and survival.

These shortcomings are based in fear and only God can love us enough to remove them from our inner world.

Notes

Meditation
Meeting the Angel of Justice

Close your eyes and find a comfortable position. Take some deep breaths, breathing from your abdomen not your chest. With each breath you feel more peaceful, more centered.

You find yourself in a circular movie theatre. You see an Angel of light motion to you to sit in one of the seats. The theatre is empty, except for you and the Angel. There is a movie screen that is big and surrounds you.

The screen is blank until the Angel sits beside you and then the movie begins, you see that this movie is about you.

Your childhood plays on this screen in colors you have never seen.

You feel at peace as you watch. Pleasant memories as well as painful ones present themselves on this big movie screen. You watch as the Angel changes one scene to another. There seems to be a balance in your scene's, a pleasant one, a painful one. You see your life up on the screen as you never have before. Different ages, different places and people.

You look at the Angel and she nods her head.

You feel relieved and freer somehow.

You watch the movie until the Angel stops the show. When the screen is once again blank you thank this Angel and come back into the room where you began, feeling awake and relaxed as you open your eyes.

Angel of Peace

The Angel of Peace reminds you of all that you know
in soft quiet whispers she speaks to your soul.
Only requesting a short time each day
so you can remember and follow the way.

Step Eight

> **Make a list of all persons we have harmed, and be willing to make amends to all of them.**

Yes, this step literally means make a list. You may want to remember the movie you watched in the last step and pull situations from the scenes.

Do not go any further than making a list, and please remember - *do not judge yourself for these incidents.* When you caused what you perceive as harm, you did the only thing you could at the time. You were being who you were.

Nothing is accomplished by beating ourselves up. That is a form of self-pity and that is not what these steps are about.

The reason for this step is the emptying of the glass and the freeing ourselves from the old ways of seeing ourselves.

Making your list and being *willing* to make amends brings us one step closer to finding peace. To free yourself from past regrets that keep you a prisoner and lock you away from your true soul's purpose is the goal.

Notes

Meditation
Meeting the Angel of Peace

Find a comfortable place to sit and take some deep breaths. In through your nose and out through your mouth. Deep breaths.

With each breath you feel more relaxed as you enter this meditation. Breathing, releasing any stress or tension you are holding on to.

Scan your whole body in your minds eye. Look to see where you are holding stress and just by recognizing, the tension lifts and it is gone. Continue to breathe normally as you see yourself in a safe place. It can be anywhere you feel safe, imagination or real, this is your place of peace.

Look around and notice where you are -
Have you ever been here before?
Do you know this place?
Is it a place you come often?
What does this place look like?
Are you outside or in?

As you become aware of your surroundings, you notice an Angel, she is so big and beautiful. She seems to be easily and peacefully floating toward you. You feel more peaceful and serene as she comes closer. You know you are being taken care of - that you are safe.

All there is happens for a reason. All that is - is right, exactly the way God planned it to be.

The Angel whispers something in your ear just loud enough for you to hear. Listen now.

You look at her and with your eyes you say thank-you. She recognizes this and nods.

When you are ready - begin to come back into the room where you began, feeling peaceful - very peaceful.

When you are ready - you can open your eyes.

Angel of Dignity

The Angel of Dignity stands straight and tall
her purpose is great, it concerns all.
She asks you to take one deep breath
and tells you your worth it, 100 percent.

Step Nine

> *Made direct amends to such people wherever possible except when to do so would injure them or others.*

Take a train, send a telegram. Find their phone number, ask a friend, write a postcard. Do some research to find these people, take a plane if you have to.

This is a gift you can give yourself. It is unlike any other gift because it can restore your self-esteem. With each acknowledgment and apology comes a gold star of dignity. When you have collected all your gold stars, your eyes will shine once again.

You will feel proud of yourself for doing the right thing and being courageous. *This is not a false pride coming from ego but true pride.* Pride of the soul. You are being humble and kind when you make amends and now that the door to the past is truly closed, you will inherit the key to the door of your future.

Notes

Meditation
Meeting the Angel of Dignity

Take some deep breaths. Begin by positioning your body so it is comfortable and not at all distracting.

Focus on the breathing - try not to have your meditation interrupted by outside noises, do this by focusing only on the breathing process. In through your nose and out through your mouth. Continue this for 10 minutes.

Now see yourself in a grand hallway, like in the old palaces of royalty, you are walking down a richly decorated long hall. You feel taller, stronger and more clear than ever before. At the end of the hallway there is a heavy gold door shining, beckoning you toward it - wanting you to come in.

You look down and notice you are walking on a red carpet. You are someone important. When you reach the door, someone opens it from the inside and you walk in.

The room is tremendous and there are many people standing around. Some you know, some you do not recognize.

The red carpet path continues as you follow it up a few stairs to a golden chair. You know you must sit in it. You feel honored as you sit and everyone is silent. They are all there to honor you and the courage you have shown.

From the left, an Angel appears, she is carrying something - you cannot quite make out what it is. The people begin clapping and calling.

The Angel stands before you, with a long ribbon to put around your neck and attached to the ribbon is a gold key. You bow your head as she puts it on. The room becomes silent again, the feeling is one of sacred gratitude. You have received the key to your soul purpose, the key to your future.

Take some time to absorb all that has occurred. When you are ready - open your eyes.

Angel of Compassion

The Angel of Compassion weaves a golden thread
from your heart to another's - not from your head
and when she is finished you will know
that this is the only right way to go.

Step Ten

> **Continued to take personal inventory and when wrong promptly admitted it.**

Just because we made amends to all those we've harmed doesn't mean we won't be wrong, make mistakes, or harm people again. But if we take a personal inventory every-day and admit or apologize right away, we will continue our journey of growth and positive change.

We must love and accept ourselves in all our glorious imperfection! With this acceptance comes the ability to love others in all their glorious imperfection as well.

Before we go to bed, we can go over our day and ask -

Did I respond the way I wanted to?
Was there something I could have done differently?
Did I react out of fear or *love?*
Did I recognize someone else's need?
Was I who I wanted to be today?
If the answer is "yes" we have lived another day for which we should be grateful.

If the answer is "no" then we need to reflect on how we could have responded or reacted and then do it differently the next time. Simple.

Also this step keeps us humble!

Meditation
Meeting the Angel of Compassion

Get comfortable and close your eyes - take a few deep breaths as you begin to feel relaxed.

Envision a pink light above your head flowing down throughout your whole body washing away any tension or stress that you are feeling. Allow this pink, loving light to surround you until you are fully embraced by it.

Now see yourself in a holy place of some kind. It can be a church or a temple, a shrine or the woods, whatever you consider a holy sacred place - be there now.

Sit down in this holy place and feel the sacredness that surrounds you. Notice the people who are there with you. One person stands out to you, seems to be connected to you - see this person now and ask this person - What do you need from me? What can I give you? Let this person answer now. Promise you will try your best to give it.

There is an Angel standing in the front of this holy place - she is holding a candle and beckons you toward her. You go and she hands you this candle. Look deep into the flame, the light that shines from this one small candle. How do you feel?

Look into the Angels eyes - what do you see?

The Angel now moves to a place where there are many candle holders and puts her candle into one. She motions for you to do the same. She tells you that each time a candle is lit with the *flame of compassion* the world gets lighter, more hopeful, more loving. You thank this beautiful Angel and you know that anytime you wish, there is another candle waiting to be lit. Because one has been lit for you.

When you feel ready, come back into this room, back into your body and open your eyes.

Angel of Communication

The Angel of Communication
talks to you fast
in ways you remember
from times long past.

Step Eleven

> *Sought through prayer and meditation to improve our conscious contact with God as we understood him, praying only for the knowledge of His will for us and the power to carry that out.*

The only way we can get to know our God better is to have contact on a daily basis with Him/Her.

When we pray, we speak to God. When we meditate, we listen. In order for us to have a whole conversation with our God, we need to speak and listen.

Many of us don't feel we have time to meditate or pray everyday. But the truth is we don't have time not to. The day goes so much better when we begin with a connection to our Higher Power.

What we are saying by this act is, "I am willing and ready for all the miracles that you have in store for me today." When we feel peaceful and centered, everyone we meet is touched in a special way and our presence in the world becomes a gift to others rather than a burden.

So take 10 minutes in the morning to say "yes."

Notes

Meditation
Meeting the Angel of Communication

Sit in a peaceful place. Put some music on and breathe, deep, slow breaths. With each breath you take you are feeling more and more aware of your inner world, more and more present in your inner world.

See yourself walking on a beach. The ocean waves are washing against the shore. The sun shines down on you as you walk and listen and feel.

You see up ahead of you caves in the rocks. Different sizes and shapes. You know which cave you wish to enter as you get closer. You step inside and it gets darker, your eyes adjust to this new place.

Standing inside is an Angel - she has been waiting for you. You both sit around a small pool of water that has formed. She is here to answer any questions that you may have now about your life. Ask some questions and allow her to answer.

Now she stands and begins to walk with you toward the opening of the cave. She tells you she will communicate with you through every-day situations and people you meet. So you must *listen wisely* to all people that you come in contact with - she will be there.

Thank her as you walk outside and squint at the sun. She waves and says *remember I will be there* - listen with your heart - you wave and take the walk back down the beach - walking along the shoreline listening to the ocean. It sounds different to you, clearer somehow.

You can feel God in the sound.

And when you are ready, you can come back into the room where you began - feeling awake and open to a new day.

Angel of Purpose

The Angel of Purpose waits for you to arrive
finally living a life where all can thrive.
After this day as you work and you play
know that an Angel is headed your way.

Step Twelve

> *Having had a spiritual awakening as a result of these steps, we tried to carry this message to others and to practice these principles in all our affairs.*

Well - we have arrived at the last step but like the wise man who knows he knows nothing, we know as long as we're alive, we are never finished growing.

The circle begins again.

We can go through these steps 100 times, on a 100 different levels and reach 100 different conclusions, receive 100 different teachings.

We have walked toward our purpose, we have reached to our soul, we have met the Angels and listened as they shared their words and love.

These steps, are a daily practice. In every moment of each day we must try and apply what we believe and know in all we do. It can not be like going to church on Sunday and forgetting the rest of the week or it is not true spirituality.

Carrying the message to others will be done in the way we live our lives, not with words. We don't need to preach to others about our way of walking in the world, we just need to walk it.

Meditation
Meeting the Angel of Purpose

Find your comfortable place and begin your deep breathing. When you get centered and feel you have released all that is keeping you from being completely present, see a white light above your head.

Allow this light to move down into your head and shoulders - relaxing, healing and protecting you. Now this white light moves down through your neck and chest area. Divine, healing light moves down through your abdomen, legs and feet - you are completely sealed and surrounded by this white light of divine protection.

See yourself in a green valley walking toward a hill that is directly in front of you. You feel driven by an invisible force to climb this hill - so you do - when you reach the top, you look down at the valley below.

There are many people, adults, children, men, women of all races - working, playing and laughing. As you get closer you notice some are singing and dancing. You feel joy as you approach this group of people. You feel you know all of them, you feel like you are home.

An Angel moves toward you - she is the Angel of purpose and she welcomes you to this land. You go and sing and play with the others. Feeling good, knowing you have arrived. Experience this for a few minutes.

You see others at work - you watch them - Do you feel you would like to do this work?

You explore these people and this land. The Angel watches over you.

There is meaning in this place and you feel part of this meaning.

Experience this for a few minutes.

And when you are ready you can come back into this room, into the place where you began. When you are ready you may open your eyes.

And the journey continues . . .

The Twelve Steps Adaptation

1- We admitted we were powerless over our old self - that our lives had become unmanageable.

2 - Came to believe that a Power greater than ourselves could restore us to sanity.

3 - Made a decision to turn our will and our lives over to the care of God, as we understand him.

4 - Made a searching and fearless inventory of ourselves.

5 - Admitted to God, ourselves, and to another human being the exact nature of our wrongs.

6 - We're entirely ready to have God remove all these defects of character.

7 - Humbly asked God to remove our shortcomings.

8 - Made a list of all persons we had harmed, and be willing to make amends to them all.

9 - Made direct amends to such people wherever possible, except when to do so would injure them or others.

10 - Continued to take personal inventory and when we were wrong promptly admitted it.

11 - Sought through prayer and meditation to improve our conscious contact with God, as we understood Him, praying only for knowledge of His will for us and the power to carry that out.

12 - Having had a spiritual awakening as a result of these steps, we tried to carry this message to others, and to practice these principles in all our affairs.

For other books and things to see,
check out our

website at

http://www.starwater.com

aah-ha! Books, Inc
PO Box 488
12 Virginia Ct
Amityville, NY 11701
Toll Free: 1-888-238-1548
Tel: 631-598-8842
Fax: 631-691-1357
e-mail: staff@starwater.com

Help for Hard Times, Clear and Simple®
aah-ha! Books, Inc.
New York